THE SHUM SHUMS NEW CHUMS

Rich McWatt
Illustrated By Calvin Innes

R McWatt Publishing

R McWatt Publishing
43 Beverley Road . Dunswell . HU6 0AD

Copyright © 2015 Rich McWatt

Illustrations & Cover by Calvin Innes.

First Print 2015
by R McWatt Publishing
Printed in the United Kingdom

ISBN-13: 978-0-9932248-1-2

British library Cataloguing in Publication Data
A CIP catalogue record for this book is available from the British Library

www.theshumshums.co.uk

Dedicated To
Nikkie and Evie, for all your support,
love and belief in me.

"Oh where is Kegger, where could she be?"
A note of concern from her dad, Little G.

Blurbo Sayer heard the commotion and ran to the scene.
He found out what had happened, but what did it mean?

Meanwhile, Kegger was sitting as
her ankle had been hurt.
She had tripped trying to run in
her long, flowing skirt.

When she fell she slipped through a hidden gap in a rock. She looked at her ankle which had swollen out of her sock!

'Where has she gone? We have looked everywhere!
Little G's worry had changed the colour of his hair.

Dependant on mood, a Shum Shums hair colour will change,
from green to red, black to yellow, it's all very strange.

At the moment Little G's was a deep dark black, meaning he was so worried, he just wanted his girl back.

Kegger and Toddy strolled into his town,
he introduced her to all the folk and showed her around.

Toddy was also thinking the same,
He was even trying out Kegger with his surname.

"Toddy and Kegger Todd, I pronounce you man and wife"
Toddy was thinking that would be such a perfect life.

The following morning the Shum Shums went looking,
to find the blue people and take some home made cooking.

They wanted to say sorry
for being so nasty,
Little G had even cooked up
his famous Cornish pastie.

So in Bloomingdale Wood, there are many different races...

...and nobody cares about the colour of their faces.